Make Him Beg to Be Yours: 14 Sneaky Steps to Win His Heart, Get Him to Commit, and Never Want to Leave You

By Dominic Mann

Table of Contents

Introduction

There are two different approaches you can take when it comes to making your guy commit. You will learn both in this book.

In the first section of this book, you will learn a powerful collection of techniques—taken straight out of some of the most hardcore psychology textbooks—that will empower you to indirectly make your man rabidly eager to lock you down while he still can.

In the second section, you will learn what men *really* want—the things that make them say to themselves, "Now *that* is girlfriend/wife material right there." (Hint: It's the stuff you'll never see mentioned in traditional women's magazines and television shows.) Some of it's rude. Some of it's crude. But like the equally rude and crude AK-47 (gun), it works every time and can take down any man.

Finally, you'll be equipped with some more advanced tips such as on how to tip the relationship dynamics in your favor, how to make him value you 10X more than he would otherwise, *exactly* what to say to him if he says he's "not ready for a relationship," and how to make him invested in a relationship and eager to "win you over".

So... if you would like to get your man to commit... even if the very *word* "commitment" or "relationship" or "girlfriend" make him tense up and quickly change topic... then dive right in to make that man putty in your hands.

PART I: The Stick

The carrot and the stick are to be used in conjunction—
just as a cart driver both dangles a carrot in front of the mule
and holds a stick behind it.

Why He Won't Commit

You're in quite the dilemma. Your man is getting all of his needs met. You do everything for him. You're basically his girlfriend, sans the title.

But for you, however, the story is quite different. You're not getting your needs met. You want *more*. You want to know where the two of you stand. You want commitment.

Put simply, he's getting his sexual (and other) needs met, without having to meet your commitment needs.

It's not that he's Dr. Evil and trying to string you along. He simply has no reason to commit.

Commitment is a big thing for men. And so if there's no reason to commit, then it ain't gonna happen.

If we view relationships as social exchanges (which,

essentially, they are), then the particular exchange you've currently got set up is not in your favor. You've given everything you've got and have nothing left to bargain with.

I know, I know. This sounds like a terribly simplistic and cold-hearted way of viewing things. But bear with me. This perspective yields lessons that can help you nudge him toward commitment.

So if relationships really are social exchanges—an unspoken give-and-take agreement—then how can you "renegotiate" it? How can you "even up" what is currently an uneven exchange?

Well girl, you're in luck, because there are four influence principles you can use to balance the scales and nudge your man toward commitment. (Yes, *nudge*, you can't "make him" or, God forbid, "force him".)

So pull out your notepad and put on your reading glasses because here they are...

The 4 Keys To Getting Commitment

#1. Be Less Interested

No. Not like *that*. Don't take this (or anything I say, for that matter) to the extreme. I don't mean flush your phone down the toilet, get on the next flight to Kenya, and never see him again.

No. What I mean is that you're likely too invested in this relationship. You're the one putting in all the effort. You're the one who's always interested, who responds to text messages in less than 30 seconds, and answers calls on the first ring. Meanwhile, he's likely putting in relatively little effort.

What this leads to is an imbalanced relationship. You (likely) value it more than he does—at least at this point.

You need to take a bit of a step back. Try being a touch less needy (or, if you're *really* needy—be a helluva lot less needy).

It really comes down to this: The least desperate person, the person who's more willing (and able) to walk away, has the power to guide the relationship. And if you're needy and desperate, you get what you're given—not what you want.

So... be less interested. At least for now. Stop immediately responding to texts. Stop waiting around for him to finalize plans at the last minute. Stop being needy, clingy, and desperate (if this applies to you). Just stop it. Bring it down a notch.

Be less interested and see how he responds.

Anyhow, this leads us right to the next influence principle...

#2. Make Yourself Scarce

In other words, stop being so damn available!

You're not a corner convenience store. You don't need to be available 24/7. Quite the contrary, in fact. It's better if you're *not*.

When you stop being available 24/7, you give him the chance to truly appreciate you. To miss you, even.

Just as the family pet gets the most cuddles and pats when it becomes apparent it needs to be put down (i.e. euthanized), and a celebrity sells the most albums the week after they die, so too do you become more highly valued and appreciated when you're scarcer.

Now, once again, cancel that flight to Kenya. That's not what I mean.

Instead, just start being less available. I know, that's the last thing you want to do. But if he's not willing to commit, there's no point you devoting all your time to him. That's girlfriend stuff. (Even then it's important to live your own life, but that's a lesson for another time.)

When you're no longer available 24/7 and constantly

tending to his needs, he'll almost certainly feel the loss. As a result, his desire for you will increase—and, in turn, so will his willingness to commit.

However, if he doesn't seem to care that you're less available (and, as of #1, less interested), then he's most likely just "not that into you" and doesn't value you. In this case, he may see you as a "placeholder" until he eventually finds "The One" (not you).

Anyhow... onto more cheerful matters.

The actionable takeaway from this section?

You're not his servant, so stop acting like one! Be less available, become scarcer, and he'll value you more.

Incidentally (or not), this leads right into the next influence principle...

#3. Create Some Competition

He hasn't committed to you (unfortunately). What this

means is that you shouldn't be 100 percent invested in him. That's girlfriend stuff. And, as far as he's concerned, that you are not.

So don't be afraid to date other guys. If he's not committing, that's fine. If he's "not ready" to be exclusive or "official", that's fine.

But that does not mean that *you* should be committed and exclusive. Once again, that's girlfriend stuff. And if you're acting like his girlfriend already, what need does he have to commit?

If he wants exclusivity, that's fine. But the relationship needs commitment.

So, until that happens, go date other guys. Broaden your social network. Create competition and (dare I say it?) even a little jealousy.

Now, before you brush off this piece of advice—dating other guys, that is—as nonsense, I strongly urge to you reconsider. If you're seeking commitment from your guy (else why are you reading this book?), **dating other men might just be the single most powerful thing you can do to inspire his commitment.**

So...

Date other men.

Exclusivity requires commitment. (Heck, back in the old days, women almost always kept dating several other guys until they got a ring on their finger (i.e. engagement), at which time they had to pull out their pen and paper and write "Dear [insert name of the guys they were dating]...".)

Although you might wish it were otherwise, the fact of the matter is...

Exclusivity does *not* lead to commitment.

Quite the opposite. In fact...

Dating other men will inspire *more* passion from him.

Moreover, this will help with influence principles #1 and

#2 (*Be Less Interested* and *Make Yourself Scarce*).

As counterintuitive as it may seem:

- Make a man the center of your world and he starts to feel less romantic about you.

- Date other guys and you'll inspire more passion and willingness to commit.

Anyhow...

You, being the astute reader you are, probably noticed how this links right back into the previous influence principle—#2—regarding scarcity. Heck, it even links into #1—*Be Less Interested*.

You see, all of these influence principles go hand in hand. They work together.

And why is it that they're just so darn effective?

People value more what they think they might lose.

So start dating other guys.

#4. Get Him To Invest

"He that has once done you a kindness will be more ready to do you another, than he whom you yourself have obliged."
– Benjamin Franklin

Once upon a time, U.S. founding father Benjamin Franklin turned a nasty political adversary into a close friend.

How did he do it, you ask?

By asking him if he would be so kind as to lend him a book.

(The man had an extensive library, and Franklin knew he had one book he prized above all others—which Franklin asked to borrow.)

But... why did that change anything?

After all, he's just lending a book. What's it matter?

Well, it turns out there's some serious psychology behind it.

You see, our subconscious cannot reconcile two opposing beliefs—such as hating somebody but doing them a favor. And so the person starts to view the person for whom they did the favor more favorably.

They become invested.

As Benjamin Franklin himself observed in the above quote, having somebody do you a favor makes them like you *more* than if *you* had done a favor for them. Seems absurd, but it's true.

So how can you apply this to nudging your man toward commitment?

Simple. **Ask him to do things for you.**

At the moment, you're likely more invested in him than he is in you. Even it up by getting him to invest more in the relationship. Every now and then, ask him to do you a favor. Because **the more he invests in the relationship, the more you will mean to him.**

So stop doing favors and start asking for them.

(Note: Once again, don't take this to the extreme. No guy wants an overly demanding or high maintenance girl.)

The actionable takeaway?

Get him to fix something, give you a ride, grab a soda from the fridge, study with you—anything!

The more time, effort or work he puts toward you, the more personally invested he becomes. And the more invested he is in you, the more you will mean to him, the more he will like you, and the more he will be willing to commit.

PART II: The Carrot

The carrot and the stick are to be used in conjunction—
just as a cart driver both dangles a carrot in front of the mule
and holds a stick behind it.

Become The Woman He Wants To Commit To

Napoleon Bonaparte once said, "Men are moved by two levers only: fear and self interest."

In the previous section we discussed how people value more what they think they might lose and how you can use related influence principles to nudge your man toward commitment. Or, put more simply, we discussed using the "lever" of fear.

Now we shall explore the other component to this equation: Self-interest. In other words, you need to be a woman he wants to commit to. If you're not somebody he wants to commit to, he isn't going to be moved by the possibility of losing you.

So how do you become the type of woman he wants to

commit to?

Simple. You make him happy. You make his life better than it would be were it not for you. Because guess what? If he's not happy or he thinks he'd be happier alone or with another woman, then why on Earth would be commit to you?

This brings us to the following question: *How do you make him happier?*

Well, there's a few components to this, but it all comes down to this: You give him what he wants, when he wants it.

Now before you get up in arms and start a feminist revolt, realize that relationships are a give-and-take affair. Most men try to make their women happy, and they expect (or at least *want*) the same in return. Whether it's a more traditional marriage where the man is the breadwinner and the woman is the homemaker, or [another example], this rule always applies. It's give-and-take.

Give your man what he really wants and you might just find that he gives you what *you* really want: A close, connected relationship.

Anyway, let us get back to the topic at hand: Making your man *want* to commit.

You see, there's this big myth that men hate commitment. While it's true that men are more resistant to commitment than women, the idea that they will never commit is ridiculous (just look up annual marriage statistics).

The truth is that a man will more than happily commit if he thinks she's the right woman.

So what do men want? How do you make his life better, easier, and happier? (Hint: Give him what he wants, when he wants it.)

Well, men have a few needs/wants that need to be met for him to even begin thinking about commitment. Let's take a look at them...

PHYSICAL

Be Sexy

Yes, men love sex. It's no secret.

What might be a secret though (especially if you've been reading all those glossy women's magazines at the grocery store checkout) is the fact (yes, *fact*) that a woman's physical appearance is the number one factor when it comes to male attraction.

No, it's not because all men are superficial pigs. They're just hardwired that way.

(To cut a long story short, in evolutionary times, men who were attracted to healthy-looking, fertile young women out-reproduced men who were attracted to ugly, disabled, infertile old ladies. Because the guy's baby is going to grow inside her body, her physical traits matter. But for women, it was a man's behavior—strong, confident, dominant, masculine, etc.—that best increased the odds of successfully reproducing as he could protect the vulnerable, pregnant woman and the weak infant and fight off those big scary sabertooth tigers. Hence, women don't place such a premium on a man's looks. But I digress.)

So what does all of this mean for you?

Simple. Look good.

While I know you can't change your genetics, you *can* change that mushy belly fat, cellulite, and jiggly tuckshop arms (if applicable). If you're already in great shape, make sure to always look your best. If you put no effort into your appearance, have no makeup on, have shaggy undone hair, loose pyjama pants, and a daggy shirt—then you're sabotaging your attractiveness. It would be like if your man rocked up one day with a whiny, weak, wussy cry-baby attitude. Yuck!

Funnily enough, this also links right into the first section. You see, when you look smoking hot, other guys can't help but take notice and lust after you.

And you know what that does? It makes your guy—whether consciously, subconsciously, or both—say, "Oh shoot, I better lock this baby down before another guy snags her."

Anyway...

So we've got looks out of the way. Make sure you look your best.

Now...

Blow His Mind In The Bedroom

Moving on, there is, of course, another component of pleasing your man physically: Blow his mind in bed. Rock his world (and bed). Try give him a heart attack. (Okay, maybe not that far, but you get the point.)

Fortunately, you likely have an advantage in this area.

You see, super-hot babes are often *terrible* in bed because they've just relied on their looks alone their entire life. Because their smoking hot, they think they can just lay there like a starfish.

While hot women can often get away with this because their looks save the day, you can turn this to your advantage by f*cking your man like a pornstar.

So get good in bed. Know what he likes and give it to

him. Try new things, experiment with new positions, and don't be afraid to get a little freaky. As the saying goes, be a lady on the streets but a freak in the sheets.

Keep His Belly Full

"Keep his belly full and his balls empty and you'll never lose the guy."
– Ben Settle

No, I'm not telling you to become a submissive servant or act like a stereotypical 50's housewife. But in a world where a good lay ain't hard to come by, the ability to cook up a good meal every now and then certainly sets you apart. And because most of today's young women have no clue how to cook anything other than two-minute noodles, the ability to cook gives you a distinct advantage.

In fact, I know guys who claim that the ability to cook is a "must have" if they're going to wife a girl.

So if you can't so much as boil an egg, it might be a good idea to up your cooking skills. While you don't need to cook him three meals a day seven days a week, your man will undoubtedly love the occasional home-made meal. And if there's any leftovers he takes to work the next day, you can be sure he's thinking about you.

Finally, you might just find that—like a stray cat—once you feed him, he'll just keep on coming back.

PSYCHOLOGICAL

<u>Be Feminine And Make Him Feel Like A Man</u>

Not only should you strive to make him feel good physically, but you should also strive to make him feel good psychologically.

If a woman emasculates her man, drains him of his confidence, shoots down his ambitions, and just overall makes him feel bad and like less of a man, then you can be certain he's not going to hang around for much longer.

So what should you do?

Do the exact opposite.

Make your man feel masculine. Encourage his dreams and ambitions. Make him feel confident, let him do manly things, and even let him "take care" of you once in awhile.

If all of this could be summed up in a single word, it would be this: Femininity.

Be feminine.

Men *love* feminine women. It's just how they're hardwired.

While men might say they're all for the empowerment of women, that doesn't mean they find "manly" women attractive.

So make your man feel respected, admired, and manly. In fact, making him feel as such actually increases his testosterone levels. Testosterone boosts his confidence, sex-drive, happiness and overall "manliness". So technically, doing this makes him subconsciously associate you with all these positive feelings, intensifying his attraction and love for you.

So show some vulnerability so he can show off his masculinity. He wants to feel needed as a *man*.

On the other hand, if you make him feel weak and small, you decrease his testosterone (i.e. the manliness hormone) levels.

You want to act as fuel for his testosterone. And you do this by making him respected, loved, and needed. So get him to take care of that scary spider. Hug his bicep and tell him it makes you feel safe. Men are hardwired to be protectors, so give him the opportunity to be a protector every once in awhile.

Be feminine, show some vulnerability, make him feel respected, admired, and manly, and he won't be able to help but love you.

Be An Accessory To His Ambitions, Not An Obstacle

Typically, men are mission-oriented. Men are usually ambitious—at least to a certain extent; they're not all Napoleons or Alexander the Greats.

A good woman (read: a woman that a man will want to

commit to) supports and encourages her man's goals and ambitions.

On the other hand, men *hate* it if their woman makes herself an obstacle to his ambitions. Don't be the woman who's constantly nagging her man to "have some more work-life balance" and "take it easy" and "don't dream too big."

Men don't want demanding women. They don't want their woman to constantly be demanding that they stop pursuing their goals and instead spend more time with her. They don't want a woman who makes silly ultimatums about how it's either her or his dreams. They don't want a woman who demands that he make her the centre of his life.

In fact, all of this is one of the *biggest reasons* that men are scared to commit. They feel like if they commit then they're giving up their freedom. That they won't be able to pursue their goals, dreams, and ambitions—or worse, their woman will demand he give them up and make her the centre of his life instead. Because of this, they can see commitment as akin to a life prison sentence.

These are all the thoughts floating around in the minds of men—either consciously, subconsciously, or both—when women try to get them to commit. And it scares them sh*tless. If they so much as *think* you might be like that, they're going to run for hills as hard and fast as they can.

So what should you do?

Understand that men are different to women.

Most (yes, *most*, so don't get offended if this isn't you) women view relationships as the most important thing in their lives. There's a reason they say that walking down the aisle is the most special day in a woman's life. There's a reason that women gossip about other people's relationships.

But (most) men are different. While they value relationships, they don't value them to the same extent as women. Relationships—and the woman they're with—are secondary to their *mission*. Their higher purpose. Their dreams, ambitions, goals, whatever you want to call it.

And you need to understand that and show him that you

won't try to change him or impose yourself on his life. That you will not only accept his ambitions rather than demand he prioritize you above them, but that you will actively support, motivate, and encourage him to pursue them.

If you do that, your man may just think that you're the greatest thing that ever happened to him.

If you *don't* do that, you'll become that "crazy, needy, demanding woman" he used to date that he warningly tells his friends about. (And, in the process, making them scared of commitment too.)

It's All About Investment

No, I'm not talking stocks and bonds. You don't need to live on Wall Street to reap the rewards of investment.

So what is investment? And what does it have to do with getting your guy to commit?

Investment is basically just a way to describe how much time, effort, emotion and even money you put into a relationship.

Don't Invest Too Quickly

Too many women make the mistake of overinvesting too early in the relationship. They see a guy they like, they feel great attraction for him, and so they go all in on the relationship. They become fully invested. They think that if they fully invest on the get go and put their heart into the relationship then the guy will reciprocate by doing the same and committing.

Sounds great, right?

Unfortunately it doesn't work that way.

What you need to do instead is start off by investing only a *little*. When he does the same, invest a little more. And when he does the same, invest a little more. And so on.

Don't make the mistake of investing 100 percent in one go. Because if you do, you don't give your guy a chance to invest himself in the relationship. And if he's not invested in the relationship, he won't commit.

To summarize this into a simple maxim for you to follow:

Don't fully invest yourself without getting anything in return.

That said, don't make the mistake of going to the opposite extreme.

But... Don't Be Cold And Indifferent

This doesn't mean you should pull out your calculator and calculate the seconds, cents, and calories (read: energy) he's put into the relationship and do the exact same.

Don't become cold, calculating, and aloof. You want to be warm, open, and feminine... just don't fully commit and start acting like his girlfriend before he's even had the chance to invest.

You see, one of the mistakes women make is that they're not open with their guys. They make assumptions and don't share their concerns... until, that is, all of these bottled up emotions burst and kill the relationship. There's a reason they say that communication is the key to a good relationship. It's true.

So if you have concerns, voice them. Don't be pushy, demanding, aggressive, or put pressure on him. But don't be the girl that makes ungrounded assumptions without ever sharing her concerns with the guy, and starts becoming passive aggressive or just leaves based on an assumption that was actually probably totally without basis.

So if you're feeling worried, concerned, or upset that your guy has starting disappearing for days on end without contacting you, or seems to be less enthusiastic, or whatever it is that's bothering you—even minor things—then ask him what's up. Don't be aggressive. Don't be accusatory. Don't be angry. Don't make ultimatums or get all emotional. Just have an adult conversation. In most cases, you'll find that whatever it is was really nothing at all. Moreover, your guy will begin to feel more comfortable being honest about what his concerns are. So it's a win-win.

So be honest about what you want. Be honest about what your concerns are. Make sure (with 110 percent certainty) to not put pressure on him or be pushy or in any way.

Be Worth It

We had a conversation about this earlier, but it's worth repeating: Are you worth it? Is your guy's life dramatically better with you in it? Or would he be happier single?

This is harsh and you need to be brutally honest. Because if you're not worth it—from his perspective—there's no way you're going to get him to commit.

On the other hand, if you bring him a lot of happiness and if his life is significantly easier and better with you in it, then getting him to commit is a non-issue.

So what does this mean for you?

It means you need to get real with yourself. If you're not bringing a lot of worth and value to the relationship, you need to realize this and work on yourself. If having you in his life is not a more positive experience than being single, he won't commit.

Put simply, you need to be worth it.

<u>Make Him Earn It</u>

If you went to a casino and won $1,000 in a matter of minutes, what would you do?

If you're like most people, you'd probably just blow it.

You might buy a bunch of expensive drinks for your friends to celebrate whatever it is you're doing. You might go on a shopping spree and buy a bunch of useless stuff you don't need. You might gamble some more and lose it all.

You blow it.

On the other hand, what would you do if you had to earn that $1,000 by laboring away for minimum wage at McDonalds?

You'd carefully save it all and put it in a safe bank account. You're not going to blow that money when you had to work so hard to earn it. You value it so much more than if you'd just won it at the casino without putting in any time or effort.

Well, guess what?

It's the same when it comes to relationships.

If the guy gets you without needing to invest any time or energy to win you (and your affection) over, he's going to blow it.

On the other hand, if the guy invests a lot of time and energy into winning you and your affection over, guess what? He's going to value it so much more. He's not only going to make sure he doesn't blow it, but he's going to be committed.

It comes down to this:

A man needs to make that investment and invest himself in a woman before he commits. If he doesn't make that investment, he won't commit.

Men don't ask themselves, "Wait a sec, have I invested? Oh shoot, I haven't. Won't worry about commitment then..."

No. It's just a subconscious things. It's psychology. He values that which he has had to earn. So make him earn it and don't give yourself over without him earning it first.

Not Sure? Use The Mirror Effect

If you're confused about how to act with your man, simply mirror what he does.

So if he starts investing more time and energy into the relationship, so too do you.

If he says he loves you, then so to do you. (Only if it's true, of course.)

And so on.

Mirror his actions, effort, and overall investment and you can't go wrong. This is especially useful if you're way over-invested in him while he puts in comparatively little effort.

What To Say If He Explicitly Says He's "Not Ready For A Relationship"

So you've brought up the topic of where you are with your guy and whether it's officially a serious relationship.

But... he says he's "not ready for a relationship."

It happens to the best of women. So how should you respond? What should you say?

There are four things you want to make clear in your response:

1. That it seems like he should go away and spend some time figuring out what he wants.

2. That you want nothing more in the world than his

happiness, and that's why you feel like he needs some time alone to figure out what he wants.

3. That you hope you're still around by the time he comes back and is ready.

4. That you want someone who is 100 percent certain about wanting to be with you.

This style of response was laid out by Matthew Hussey (www.matthewhussey.com). Here are the exact words Hussey suggested women use when a man tells you he's "not ready for a relationship":

"It seems like you need to go away and figure out what you want and be on your own for a while. And I want your happiness more than anything in the world. I just you want you to be happy. So I feel like you need to go and be alone in order to figure out what you want. And I hope that I'm here or that I'm still here when you're ready. But until then I know that I need someone who is completely in because I wouldn't want to be with someone who isn't 100 percent about wanting to be with me."

(NOTE: This is only if he's not ready for a relationship after a few months *at least.* Don't whip this out on him on the first date.)

Why is it that this response is so effective?

It's because of its four components.

Firstly, when you make it clear that it's *okay* by telling him he's right and needs to go be on his own makes him scared. He almost certainly doesn't want to go and be on his own. Moreover, because you're agreeing and making it *okay* for him, he has nothing to rebel against. It's not as if he feels he's being forced to run because you're aggressively trying to box him into a relationship.

Secondly, when you tell him that you care for his happiness and that it means the world to you... I mean, come on. He sees that as coming from such a loving, sweet, pure place. He now sees an unbelievably loving woman in front of him he's about to lose.

Thirdly, saying that you hope you're still here when he's

ready puts that fear of loss in his mind—he doesn't want to lose you.

Finally, saying that you want someone who is 100 percent sure about you shows that you have standards and you know what you deserve. It shows your value and it shows you respect yourself. And although you love him, you also love yourself—and so you can't settle for anything less than a man who's completely sure about you.

All in all, it's a response that's very loving, kind, and strong. It makes him realize you're a woman he's truly going to be losing out on in a big way in his life.

Conclusion

To wrap up this book, I want to address an issue you might otherwise struggle with.

You see, you might be thinking...

"Well all of this is well and good, but doesn't the second half of the book contradict the first half?"

"You say be less available and use all those other influence principles to 'nudge him toward commitment', and then you're telling me to 'rock his world', 'f*ck him like a pornstar', make him feel manly, and be his biggest supporter?"

"You're telling me to go left and then right? To feed him a carrot then whack him with a stick?"

If you're a little confused, that's understandable.

Although it may at first seem that these are two irriconoscibile pieces of advice, they actually go hand in hand.

That which is with us all the time is invisible to us. That's why you virtually forget you're wearing clothes or that you have a tongue in your mouth. And so in the first section we had a conversation about how you can make your man more willing to commit by helping him realize how much he values you—such as by giving him room to miss you.

Then we talked about how to be the most amazing thing that ever happened to him *while you are with him.*

See how these two seemingly contradictory perspectives work together to pack the ultimate punch?

Rock his world when you're with him. And let him miss you when you're gone.

—

P.S. I would advise reviewing some of the key points in this book a few times. (It is for this purpose that I have made the book as short and snappy as possible rather than bloating it with long stories, inactionable information, and other fillers.) If it works best for you, try implementing one point at a time.

I wish you the very best.

Printed in Great Britain
by Amazon